Fill a bucket®

A Guide to Daily Happiness for Young Children

By Carol McCloud and Katherine Martin, M.A.
Illustrated by David Messing

Ferne Press

Authors' Acknowledgments:

Our deepest gratitude to Dave Messing, whose delightful and colorful illustrations bring the bucketfilling concept to life; to our publisher Marian Nelson, who trusted in the idea since the beginning; to our young editor Kasey Walsh, for her suggestions; and, most importantly, to Him who commands us to "love one another" or "fill a bucket" because He knows what's good for us.

In the 1960s, Dr. Donald O. Clifton (1924-2003) first created the "Dipper and Bucket" story that has now been passed along for decades. Dr. Clifton later went on to coauthor the *#1 New York Times* bestseller *How Full Is Your Bucket?* and was named the Father of Strengths Psychology.

A portion of the proceeds from this book is being donated to the Methodist Children's Home Society in Redford, Michigan, which has served abused and neglected children since 1917.

Summary: The concept of a full bucket is an effective metaphor for a child's healthy self-concept and happiness, most often the result of the encouraging words and actions of parents and others who help a child know they are loved, valued, and capable.

Library of Congress Cataloging-in-Publication Data
McCloud, Carol and Martin, Katherine
Fill a Bucket: A Guide to Daily Happiness for Young Children – First Edition
ISBN: 978-1-933916-43-9
1. Child Development 2. Parenting 3. Behavior 4. Kindness 5. Happiness
I. McCloud, Carol and Martin, Katherine II. Fill a Bucket: A Guide to Daily Happiness for Young Children
Library of Congress Control Number: 2009930997

FERNE PRESS

Ferne Press is an imprint of Nelson Publishing & Marketing
366 Welch Road, Northville, MI 48167
www.nelsonpublishingandmarketing.com
(248) 735-0418

Fill a Bucket®

Tune: *Frère Jacques* or *Are You Sleeping?*

1. Fill a buck - et Eve - ry day
2. Fill a buck - et Eve - ry day

I can fill a buck - et You can too
I like fill - ing buck - ets You will too

1. Fill a bucket. (Fill a bucket.)
   Every day. (Every day.)
   I can fill a bucket. (I can fill a bucket.)
   You can too. (You can too.)

2. Fill a bucket. (Fill a bucket.)
   Every day. (Every day.)
   I like filling buckets. (I like filling buckets.)
   You will too. (You will too.)

The day you were born was a very happy day.
It was your birthday, a day you celebrate every year.

You were a new person and a special gift. You received a gift too—your very own name, a name as special as you. What is your name?

Everyone was so happy to see you.
But, there was one part of you that they could not see.
It was your bucket, your invisible bucket.

Everyone is born with an invisible bucket. No one can see your bucket, but it is always with you. Your bucket is a very important part of you. It is an important part of everyone.

Your bucket holds all the love and happiness that you receive
each day. When your bucket is full, you feel happy.
When your bucket is empty, you feel sad.
It's good to have a full bucket.

Every day, your family and lots of other people help fill
your bucket. When your daddy kisses and tickles you,
he fills your bucket. Your giggles fill his bucket, too.

When your mommy smiles and tells you she loves you, she is filling your bucket. Your smiles fill her bucket, too.

When your sister or your brother snuggles and reads to you,
your buckets fill up even more.

When your grandpa or your grandma plays with you,
everyone's bucket is filled.

Look! Your bucket is so full! It is full of happy thoughts and lots of love. So many people have filled your bucket. You can fill their buckets, too.

Bucket filling is like magic. When you fill a bucket by being kind and loving, your bucket fills up, too.

You can do many things to fill buckets every day.
When you listen and help, you are filling a bucket.
Your bucket fills up more.

When you say "please" and "thank you,"
your magic words fill buckets.

When you play and share your toys, everyone is happy.
Everyone's invisible bucket is filled.

When you take care of your pet, you are filling a bucket.
Your bucket fills up, too.

When you smile and wave, you are being a bucket filler.

When you give hugs and kisses, your love fills buckets. It's good to go to sleep with a bucket full of happiness and love.

Look! Look at all the happy faces.
Everyone's bucket is full.

Now it's your turn.

What will you do to fill a bucket?

About the Authors

Carol McCloud is an early childhood specialist, popular speaker, and president of Bucket Fillers, Inc., an educational organization in Brighton, Michigan. Her first book, *Have You Filled a Bucket Today? A Guide to Daily Happiness for Kids,* was published in May of 2006. Since then, she and her team of Bucket Filler educators have traveled across the United States giving school assemblies and staff development seminars. For information on presentations, books, and other bucketfilling products or to receive the free e-newsletter, BUCKET FILL-OSOPHY 101, visit www.bucketfillers101.com.

Katherine Martin, M.A., is a youth and adolescent specialist, Bucket Filling teammate, and frequent contributor to the bucketfilling newsletter. In late 2007, she joined Carol in writing *Fill a Bucket: A Guide to Daily Happiness for Young Children* for parents and teachers of younger children to help them learn and teach the joy of filling buckets.

About the Illustrator

David Messing is a life-long artist, illustrator, cartoonist, sculptor, writer, and instructor. For twenty-five years, Dave has taught at his family-owned business, Art 101. Dave also designs and builds props, sets, and miniatures for print and film commercials. His work can be seen on TV, billboards, in national magazines, and in movies. Please visit www.davemessing.741.com.

If you enjoyed this book, you will also enjoy *Have You Filled a Bucket Today?*

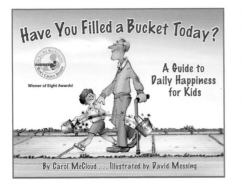

2007	Mom's Choice Awards – Best Children's Picture Book
2007	Writer's Digest Self-Published Book Awards – Best Children's Picture Book
2007	DIY Book Festival – Best Children's Picture Book
2007	Books-and-Authors.net – Best Children's Picture Book
2007	Best You Can Be Foundation – Top 10 Children's Books
2007	London Book Festival – Honorable Mention
2008	Nautilus Book Awards – Silver Medal
2008	NABE Pinnacle Book Achievement Award
2011	Purple Dragonfly Award